Goal Setting and Getting Things Done

90 Minute Guides

Michelle N. Halsey

Silver City Publications & Training, L.L.C.
P.O. Box 1914
Nampa, ID 83653
https://www.silvercitypublications.com/shop/

ISBN-10: 1-64004-022-6
ISBN-13: 978-1-64004-022-9

Contents

Chapter 1 – Overcoming Procrastination

Everyone has dreams and goals. Achieving personal and professional goals, however, requires planning and action. Learning how to manage time and set realistic goals will increase your chance of success in every area of your life. Following the advice in this course will help increase your productivity and help you achieve your dreams.

At the end of this chapter, you should be able to:

- Overcome procrastination

- Manage time effectively

- Accomplish important tasks

- Self-motivate

- Create SMART goals

Before reading through this chapter, review the following questions and note your responses.

- How would you describe your goal setting and time management process?

- Have you ever taken a course in goal setting? What was the focus?

- Where do you feel your skills are weak?

- What do you hope to learn from this course?

Overcoming Procrastination

We all procrastinate from time to time. Procrastination occurs when we avoid tasks that we find unpleasant. Even if we perform other work-related tasks instead of the ones we dislike, we are guilty of procrastination. Unfortunately, procrastination will hinder our long-term success. With the proper skills, you can overcome procrastination.

Eat That Frog!

Mark Twain has a saying that applies to procrastination:

If the first thing you do each morning is to eat a live frog, you can go through the day with the satisfaction of knowing that that is probably the worst thing that is going to happen to you all day long!

Brian Tracy named his course on time management "Eat that Frog" because of this saying. The frog is anything that you do not want to do. Basically, you should complete your dreaded tasks first. Getting them out of the way will provide you with a sense of accomplishment and keep you from procrastinating. Always begin with the task that is the hardest and most significant, and you will be less tempted to procrastinate on other activities.

Just Do It

When you dislike a particular task, it is easy to procrastinate. Whether you spend time checking email or looking at Instagram, you are procrastinating. You need to do more than identify when you procrastinate. You need to discover why.

- Discover your obstacles: What do you choose over your tasks?

- Discover ways to remove obstacles: Ask for support, and take action. For example, you could turn off the Internet and your phone.

- Reward yourself: Make the task fun, and use small rewards as incentive.

Once you have identified your frogs and obstacles, the only answer is take action. Make the tasks that you want to avoid part of your daily routine. Schedule the tasks into your calendar. Once they become habit, you will find them easier to accomplish. Once you have scheduled the time to accomplish your tasks, you must follow through. Resist the temptation to procrastinate with your favorite time waster. Just do it.

The 15 Minute Rule

Lack of time is a common excuse for not completing a task. We often overestimate the time that it takes to complete tasks, but the 15 minute rule allows you to accurately time your tasks. When you follow the 15 minute rule, you set a timer for 15 minutes and work on a task. You should stop working on the task when the time is up. You will be surprised by how many tasks you complete within the 15 minutes. When you are not able to complete a task within 15 minutes, schedule 15 minutes the next day for the same task. This allows you to make consistent progress. You will also be able to better estimate how long a similar task will take.

Chop It Up

The size of a project can also contribute to procrastination. It is easy to become overwhelmed by a large project. The key to overcoming procrastination is to chop up the large project into smaller tasks. Rather than looking at the entire project, focus on the single task. This will prevent you from becoming overwhelmed by the enormity of the work you must complete. For example, you could break a large report into different tasks such as brainstorming, outlining, writing, etc. This technique will create a sense of achievement with each step and improve motivation, allowing you to stay focused as you reach the end of the entire project.

Procrastination can happen at any time. It is not enough to identify that you are avoiding a project. You need to take active steps to remove the temptation to procrastinate. By taking control of your schedule and work environment, you will be able to reduce the amount of time that you spend procrastinating each day. In turn, you will be able to improve your productivity and accomplish your goals.

Remove Distractions

We are bombarded with distractions every day. These distractions are temptations to procrastinate. By removing as many distractions as possible, you will be on track to overcoming procrastination.

Distractions to Avoid:

- **Office clutter**: Clean up your space at the end of each day, both at home and in the office. This will help to keep you focused, and you will not be tempted to clean during a project.

- **Email notification**: Establish specific times to check email. Automatic notifications are distracting and cut into the time you spend on each project.

- **Telephone calls**: Do not take all calls. Choose a time to return calls and texts.

- **Environment**: Remove distractions such as books, magazines, etc., from your workstation.

Start Small and Build

A habit of procrastination does not happen overnight. Equally, it is not possible to stop procrastinating overnight. Expecting an immediate change will only lead to disappointment. You need to start small and build in order to end procrastination once and for all. Begin by creating a daily "to do list" for your personal life. Include the daily tasks that you have trouble completing such as laundry or cleaning the kitchen. When you have stability in your personal schedule, it will be easier to address procrastination at work.

Create a daily schedule for work once you have broken down your larger tasks into smaller ones. As your productivity increases, you will be able to build upon your schedule. You will soon find that you are finishing tasks ahead of schedule.

Reward Yourself

People tend to procrastinate because they do not find certain tasks to be pleasant. Procrastination becomes its own reward. Overcoming procrastination requires that you implement a reward system for completing tasks. Otherwise, you will revert to bad habits. Rewards should match the tasks completed. For example, taking 10 minutes on Facebook could be a reward for returning your phone calls. Similarly, going to a movie could be a reward for completing a report on time. When choosing rewards, you need to stay away from anything that you already have planned. For example, if you already have plans to go out with friends on a weekend, the outing will not serve as a reward. Using the appropriate rewards will improve motivation and help prevent procrastination.

Set Realistic Deadlines

Schedules and deadlines will help you stay focused and avoid procrastination. When setting deadlines, however, you must be realistic. Deadlines that are not realistic will actually contribute to procrastination. If you do not have a chance of completing a task on time, you will avoid it. If you are creating your own deadline, you should consider how long similar tasks have taken. Be honest, and allow time for interruptions and emergencies. Do not create a schedule based on the best-case scenario. You are setting yourself up for failure. If you are assigned a deadline, determine if it is realistic. If the deadline is not realistic, you should attempt to negotiate a more realistic date. This negotiation should be done as quickly as possible to prevent complications later.

Chapter 2 – Four P's of Goal Setting

You need goals to get things done. However, not every goal is effective. The way that you word your goals will determine whether or not you reach them. When establishing goals, it is important to remember the **Four P's** of goal setting. They need to be positive, personal, possible, and prioritized.

They Need to Be Positive

When you are creating goals, remember to make sure that they are positive. This means that you focus on what you want to achieve rather than what you want to avoid. For example, you would write, *"I will achieve a promotion."* rather than *"I will no longer work at this horrible job."* Staying focused on the positive will help improve your outlook and remove any negativity. This, in turn, will improve your chances for success. Reaching your goals will automatically help you avoid your present circumstances. When creating positive goals, remember to be as specific as possible.

They Need to Be Personal

When creating goals, they need to reflect your dreams and desires. Goals that are not personal are ineffective. Your goals should be about you and only you. For example, *"My boss will appreciate me."* is an ineffective goal because it is not about you. It is possible to be a wonderful employee and still be unappreciated. A better goal would be, *"I will find a supervisory position where I am appreciated for my talent."* If your goals are not personal, you will never achieve them. Making goals personal places the burden of responsibility on you, but it also means that other people do not determine when you reach your goals.

They Need to Be Possible

When creating goals, you need to make sure that they are possible. When you set impossible goals, you set yourself up for failure and disappointment. Creating possible goals demands that you be honest with yourself. Some goals may require continued education or experience to achieve while others will remain out of reach. For example, it is not possible for someone to become a famous singer without any talent whatsoever. You need to assess your talents and determine what you can achieve with hard work and what will be impossible for you to accomplish. Once you have determined which goals are possible for you to achieve, success will be within reach.

They Need to Be Prioritized

Brainstorming goals can become overwhelming. You will probably have more goals than you can handle. This is the time to prioritize your goals. Begin by numerically ranking your goals and choosing the five goals that are the most important to you. Choose these goals based on your passions, and make sure that they cover all areas of your life: professional, health, personal growth, finances, etc. All of your time and energy should be spent working towards these goals.

You should place your other goals on the back burner. It is not possible to focus on 20 goals at the same time. In fact, you should avoid the other goals at all cost. You risk becoming side tracked with less important goals if you continue to entertain them. You will need to reprioritize your goals periodically. For example, you can reprioritize after you achieve one of your top five goals.

Chapter 3 – Improving Motivation

Goals can be inspiring, but that inspiration can fade in the reality of everyday life. In order to achieve your goals, it is important that you find ways to motivate yourself. You cannot constantly rely on external motivation. Implementing different methods of motivation such as remembering peak moments, writing down goals and gamification will help keep you stay focused and positive as you work towards your goals.

Remember Peak Moments

Positive memories are powerful motivators. Remembering peak moments creates the sense of achievement and encourages us to seek out that same feeling again. Peak moments are not relegated to work accomplishments. They are any strong memories that create positive feelings. For example, completing a marathon may be a peak moment. Getting married or having a child can also be peak moments. Looking back over your peak moments will show you how much you already have, and how far you have already come. They will encourage and motivate you to keep moving forward and reach your goals.

Write Down Your Goals

Knowing your goals is not enough to keep you motivated; you have to write them down. Writing down goals creates a visual reminder of where you are going. When you are writing down your goals, remember to:

- Use the present tense or the present perfect tense: This will help you visualize reaching your goals.

- Use "I" statements: An "I" statement reinforces that they are personal goals. They are your responsibility.

Example:

- I am graduating with my Master's degree.

Once your goals are written down, you should display them someplace where you will see them regularly.

Use Gamification

Gamification uses the process of game dynamics to blend intrinsic and extrinsic motivation. Unlike online games that can become obstacles to productivity, gamification will actually help you achieve your goals. This system allows you to earn points towards rewards by accomplishing tasks. The points you earn provide incentives to complete more tasks and earn more rewards. You can create your own life game by taking a few steps.

Create Your Own Game:

- **Identify tasks:** List the tasks/chores that you need to accomplish.

- **Assign points**: Assign a number of points to each task. Tasks that you typically avoid should be given more points to provide greater incentive.

- **Assign rewards:** Determine how many points are necessary to earn each reward. Higher point counts should be given to rewards that are more valuable. For example, an outing to a coffee shop could be 20 points, while purchasing game, book, etc., could be 120 points. The rewards will depend on what motivates you.

- **Keep score:** Find a method to keep track of your points that works for you. You could use a spreadsheet or list them in an app on your phone.

You will probably have to adjust your game to find the most motivating rewards system. Once you have made the necessary adjustments, you will have fun reaching your goals.

Track Your Progress

Tracking your progress will help you see your accomplishments and which areas require more effort. Additionally, seeing the improvements that you make will motivate you to continue your hard work. Over time, you should see yourself consistently reaching more of your daily goals. There are different ways to track progress. You may choose to do it by hand, use a spreadsheet, or use an online tool such as Joe's Charts. No matter the format you use, charting requires you to complete a list of daily goals. At the end of each day, you check off the goals that you accomplished. Do not expect to always reach all of your goals. The purpose of tracking progress is to show you the areas need more of your focus.

Example:

Goal	Mon	Tues	Wed	Thurs	Fri	Sat	Sun
Exercise	X		X	X		X	
Journal		X			X	X	X

Chapter 4 – Wise Time Management

Time management is the key to getting things done. It is easy to become sidetracked by unimportant tasks that do not help you reach your goals without the proper time management. By following the following strategies, you will be able to navigate your time wisely. They will help you achieve your goals while decreasing your stress level and making your life easier.

Urgent/Important Matrix

In order to manage time, you need to determine the difference between urgent and important tasks. Urgent tasks are tasks that need to be done quickly, and important tasks are related to specific goals. Most tasks will be a combination of the two, such as urgent/important or urgent/unimportant. You need to place priority on important tasks, completing tasks that are both urgent and important first.

Unfortunately, we are often trapped performing urgent tasks that are not important. They may be important to the people around you, but they are distractions and interruptions that do nothing to help you meet your own goals. Important tasks should take priority because they are focused on specific goals. The urgent/important matrix below will help you identify which tasks are urgent and which ones are important.

The Urgent/Important Matrix:

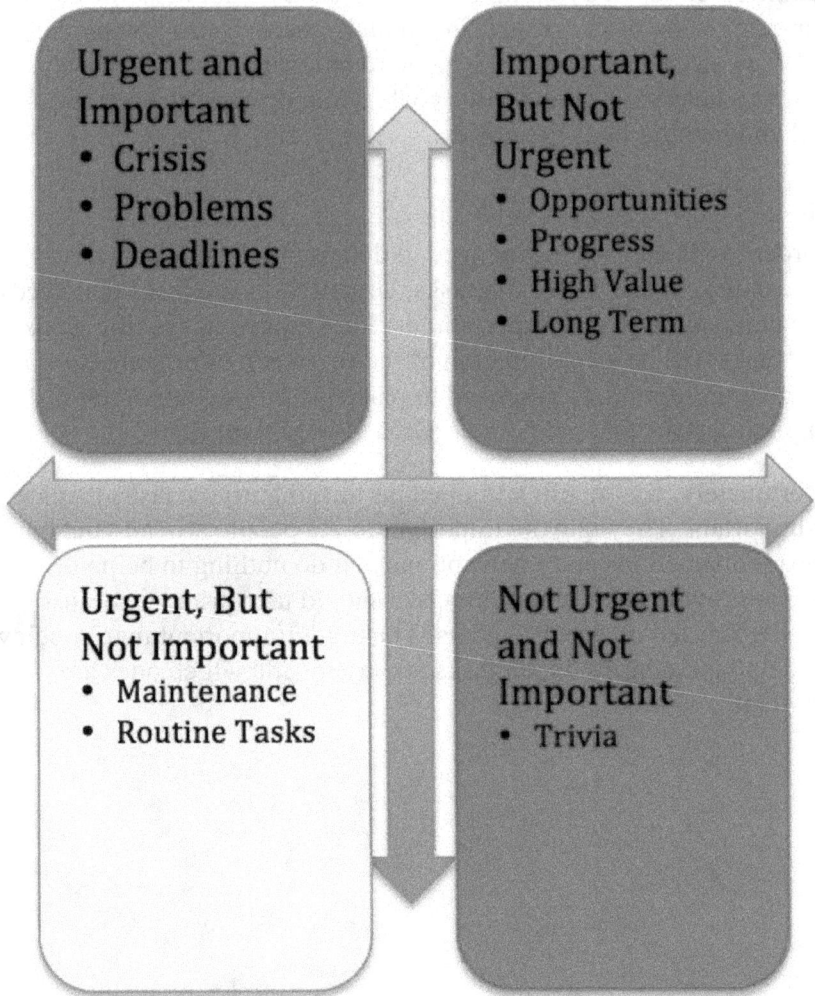

Urgent and Important	Important, But Not Urgent
• Crisis • Problems • Deadlines	• Opportunities • Progress • High Value • Long Term
Urgent, But Not Important • Maintenance • Routine Tasks	**Not Urgent and Not Important** • Trivia

The 80/20 Rule

Many successful individuals recommend following the 80/20 Rule. The 80/20 rule states that only 20 percent of our actions are responsible for 80 percent of our successes. This means that it is necessary to discover the 20 percent of our actions that are the most effective. Focus on these actions once you discover them and make them your priorities.

The 80/20 Rule should be linked to your goals. Once you prioritize goals, you should spend your most of your time working on the 20 percent of activities that you know will move you forward.

Utilize a Calendar

Calendars are essential to effective time management. Calendars are familiar tools, but they are not always used effectively. When using a calendar to manage time, it is important that you only use one. Given the different calendar options, it is easy to try to integrate different calendars, but you risk scheduling mistakes. You can choose from physical calendars, mid tech options like day-timer, and high tech apps for your phone. Find the calendar that works for you and stick with it.

Calendar Rules:

- Keep the calendar with you: Leaving the calendar behind means that you may forget to list something on it.

- Only list appointments and day events: Appointments require specific times. Events include birthdays, anniversaries, etc.

- Avoid notes: Do not clutter your calendar. Have a separate section for notes.

- Include phone numbers: While you should avoid clutter, phone numbers and addresses may be useful.

Create a Ritual

Rituals can help improve time management. Rituals are repetitive actions, which do not need to be scheduled. For example, you do not think about brushing and flossing before bed or making coffee with breakfast. By creating rituals that are connected with goals, you will not have to schedule certain tasks. For example, if you get up at the same time every morning and exercise for 30 minutes, you will create a ritual. This ritual will become a habit over time.

You will not create a ritual overnight. For the first few months, you will have to be disciplined in your efforts. It takes time to create a habit. How long it takes a habit to form will vary according to each individual. There is no magic number. You will have to continue your quest until your ritual is complete.

Chapter 5 – Tips for Completing Tasks

It is easy to begin tasks, but completing them is much more difficult. Life will always find a way to distract us from our tasks. Given how easy it is to procrastinate and avoid tasks, most people have a list of tasks waiting to be completed. As this list grows, stress levels increase. By following a few simple tasks, you will improve your chances of completing tasks and staying on track and reducing stress levels.

One Minute Rule

Everyone hates doing small, mundane tasks. They may seem unimportant, but over time, they will pile up, which will diminish focus and waste time. For example, if you do not take the garbage out regularly, it will overflow. This makes a simple task much more difficult. Implementing the one minute rule eliminates this difficult situation and protects your focus.

According to the one minute rule, if a task will only take one minute, you should complete it immediately. Examples of tasks that follow the one minute rule include: filing papers, putting clothes the in laundry hamper, and taking out the garbage. A single minute will not put you behind schedule, and following the rule will save you time in the long run.

Five Minute Rule

Schedules only help people focus and manage time when they are done correctly. A common mistake that people make when creating schedules is to make them too strict. It is not possible to plan the day down to the minute. When creating a schedule, you should follow the five minute rule. The five minute rule is simple: allow at least five minutes between scheduled tasks. This time is set aside so that you can complete small tasks that you have been avoiding or neglecting. The five minutes do more than provide time to complete small, seemingly unimportant projects. They also provide a buffer between scheduled activities, which will help keep you on schedule in case a task runs longer than you expected.

Break Up Large Tasks

Many tasks have multiple steps. These tasks may be overwhelming when you look at the complete picture. By breaking these tasks up into their basic steps, you will be able to remain focused as you work. Additionally, you will feel a sense of achievement as you complete each step in the process. An example of breaking up a large task would be cleaning out a garage.

Example:

- Sort through everything

- Remove unwanted items

- Organize the remaining items

- Put away items in their appropriate locations

Breaking down a task into manageable steps will make them much easier to manage. Additionally, you will be more likely to complete a project when you break it down into smaller tasks.

Utilize Technology

Technology has made completing tasks much easier. Computer software and online programs help you manage tasks, create reminders, and track your progress. Besides computer programs, there are countless apps now that help you make lists, keep track of schedules, and complete tasks. No matter which smartphone you have, there are apps to keep you on track such as Reminders, Outlook, and Todoist. You can make schedules, create lists, reply to email, etc. wherever you are. Find the technology that fits your lifestyle. If you try to use an app that you do not like, you will abandon your efforts completely. Before trying an app, ask your friends for recommendations and look up reviews online. You may also want to begin with free apps. With a free app, you have not lost any money if you do not find the app useful.

Chapter 6 – Increase Your Productivity

Improving your time management strategies will help increase your productivity. By improving your productivity, you will find it easier to reach your goals. Increased productivity takes time. However, as you begin to implement different strategies, you will discover which methods are effective and improve your personal and professional productivity.

Repeat What Works

There are numerous programs, hints, and tips available to help you improve productivity. The key to improvement is discovering what works and repeating actions with the appropriate tools. This requires researching and trying different strategies to determine which ones fit best with your workload and habits. For example, not everyone can use the same technology to keep a schedule. Once you determine which resources and strategies are effective, it is important to keep repeating them. There is no reason to change your routine once you have determined what works for you. Over time, the repetition will increase your productivity and help you move forward.

Get Faster

It may seem obvious, but the faster that you become, the more productive you will be. Practice and effort will help increase your speed on tasks that you perform regularly. For example, you can work on getting faster at typing, reading, walking, etc. No matter the task, just try to increase the speed a little bit at a time. There are numerous ways to help you get faster and improve your productivity.

Ways to Improve Speed:

- Games

- Tasks

- Apps

- Computer programs

Choose the method that fits best with your life and interests.

Remove "Should" from Your Dictionary

The words that you use have a greater impact on your life than you may realize. We have already discussed remaining positive by avoiding negative language. It is also important to avoid uncertainty in your language. For example, the word "should" needs to leave your dictionary. This word implies feelings of guilt because you do not plan on actually following through. For example, someone who says, "I should start exercising every morning" is not likely to start exercising. The decisive word "will" indicates a decision has been made. Saying, "I will start exercising" is making a commitment to follow through with an idea. Making this simple shift in vocabulary will commit you to action and improve your productivity.

Build on Your Successes

Success itself can become a cycle if you start small and build on your achievements. Once you have a single success, you will find the motivation to work towards more. You should start with a small success and build. Begin with the goal that is easy to reach. For example, you could begin by blogging every day for a week. Move on to another achievable goal. These successes will provide a foundation to build on as you attempt to reach more goals and success. By moving from success to success, you will be able to increase productivity in both your personal and professional life.

Chapter 7 – To Do List Characteristics

"To do" lists are staples in modern life. If "to do" lists are not done properly, they are useless. Too often, people create lists that they never come close to completing. There are characteristics that effective "to do" lists share. If your "to do" list includes these basic characteristics, you will find it easier to accomplish the tasks that you established.

Focus on the Important

The main mistake that people make when creating to do lists is making them too long. It is not possible to place every little task on a "to do" list. For a list to be effective, you must focus on the important tasks. The best method for making a "to do" list is to create a list of everything you want to accomplish and then cut that list down to a manageable size. You may want to use the urgent/important matrix to determine which tasks should make your list. Remember that an important task will align with your goals. If a task is not important enough to make the list, do not attempt to squeeze it in later. You do not want to split your attention. Focusing only on the important tasks will help you complete your to do list and reach your goals.

Chunk, Block, Tackle

When creating a "to do" list, you should keep chunk, block, and tackle in mind. The first part of this strategy should be familiar. You need to break up a large task into smaller ones.

- **Chunk:** Break projects into tasks that are 15 minutes or fewer.

- **Block:** Block out time to complete each chunk.

- **Tackle:** Tackle each specific task individually rather than looking at the entire project.

Implementing chunk, block, tackle, will motivate you to complete the project because you will feel a sense of accomplishment as you complete each chunk. When creating your to do list, include the project chunks that you have created rather than listing the project as a whole. You should also include the time estimate for each task.

Make It a Habit

You need to make "to do" lists regularly for them to be effective. Creating "to do" lists should become a habit for you. They should become second nature; you should not need to think about them. The best way to accomplish this is by creating your "to do" list at the same time each day. If you are an early riser, you may want to create your list first thing in the morning. On the other hand, many people prefer creating their lists at the end of the day so that it is ready in the morning. When you create a new "to do" list, you should transfer any unfinished tasks from your current list to the list for the next day. If you create your list at the same time each day, it will become a habit over time. Once creating the list becomes a habit, it will become faster and easier to revise your "to do" list every day.

Plan Ahead

"To do" lists will not help you reach your goals unless you implement them. Until they are executed, lists are just reminders of what you still need to accomplish. The key to using lists is to plan ahead. Take the time to prioritize and schedule your list each day. Place time estimates next to each task, so you can place them in your schedule.

How to complete the list:

- Make a schedule: Schedule the tasks on your "to do" list each day.

- Set a timer: Set a timer or an alarm for each task.

- Stay focused: Do not be sidetracked by unimportant tasks.

If you plan your day around your "to do" list, you will find yourself completing more of the tasks that you have assigned yourself and getting things done.

Chapter 8 – SMART Goals

If you cannot achieve your goals, there is a chance that you are not creating the correct goals. Whenever you create goals, you will find that following the rules for SMART goals will be easier to achieve. SMART goals are specific, measurable, attainable, realistic, and timely. When you combine the elements of SMART goals, you have a greater chance of success.

Specific

Goals need to be specific. You will not be able to reach you goals if they are broad and general because planning will be too difficult. For example, "Improve my life" is too broad. You cannot work towards this general goal. Specific goals explain what is necessary to complete a goal and guides you as you try to reach the goal. Specific goals may also identify location, requirements, and the reasoning behind the goal.

Example:

- **General goal:** Make more money.

- **Specific goal**: Earn a promotion with a pay increase.

Measurable

Goals need to be measurable in order to be effective. A measurable goal specifies the when a goal is accomplished by answering, "how much?" or "how many?" It provides measurable results. Without measurable goals, it is difficult to realize when the goal has been reached.

Example:

- **General goal:** Work on a book.

- **Measurable goal:** Write 10 pages a day of a book.

Attainable

Goals must always be attainable. It is important that you create goals that are challenging, but they still need to be within reach. When goals are unattainable, you will give up on them without even trying. The measure of a goal should always be attainable.

- **Unattainable goal**: Earn $1 million in the next three months.

- **Attainable goal:** Earn a $2 an hour raise with my next review.

Realistic

It is important that you set realistic goals. Realistic goals are directly related to your abilities. For example, a goal to reprogram the computer is not realistic if you do not have the education or experience to accomplish the task. Additionally, you need to make sure that you have access to the tools necessary to meet your goals. If a goal seems unrealistic, break it down into smaller chunks to know for certain.

Example:

- **Unrealistic Goal:** Run a marathon. (without training)

- **Realistic Goal:** Complete a marathon after training for a year.

Timely

Always create goals that have specific time frames. General goals do not establish any time frames, which means that you may continue to pursue goals that you should relinquish. Timely goals encourage you to move forward in order to meet the deadline you have established. Once a time frame has been reached, you should take the time to reevaluate the goal.

Example:

- **General goal:** Complete a computer training course.

- **Timely goal:** Complete a computer training course within the next month.

Chapter 9 – Mistakes Will Happen

No matter how well you prepare or what precautions you take, mistakes will happen. Mistakes are an essential part of life. Without them, it is not possible to fully grow and learn. When mistakes do occur, the key is to bounce back, learn from them, and move forward. If you learn from your mistakes, you are less likely to repeat them. You will also be able to guide others away from making the same mistakes you have.

Accept It

There are two ways to handle mistakes. You can deny the mistake or blame others, or you can accept it and take responsibility for your actions. Becoming defensive and making excuses will not help you grow or improve your relationship with other people. In fact, refusing to accept responsibility can eventually breed contempt between you and those around you, particularly if you are blaming them for your errors. Accepting is always the better option. It is the mature decision and a sign of integrity.

How to Accept Responsibility:

- Make an appropriate apology: Apologize for mistakes. Do not, however, grovel or become overly emotional.

- Reframe: Explain the mistake and the process that led to it. It honestly explains exactly what went wrong. Reframing may improve the way everyone views the error.

Bouncing Back

Never allow mistakes to paralyze you. Living in fear of making another mistake will stunt your personal and professional growth. Everyone makes mistakes, but successful people are able to bounce back. You will make mistakes, but you must be sure to get back on track when they occur. Keep a positive attitude in the face of mistakes. See them as opportunities for growth.

You must persevere and focus on the future. Never live in the past. The ability to bounce back after making a mistake shows that you are strong and resilient. Bouncing back will make it easier for you to regain trust after suffering the setback of making a mistake.

Adapt and Learn from Them

Mistakes are opportunities to adapt and learn. In order to learn from a mistake, you must look at the situation honestly. It is imperative that you show others you are able to adapt and change in the face of mistakes. This skill will help you preserve your reputation. You will also be able to provide valuable advice and prevent those around you from repeating your errors. This ability transforms your mistake from a liability to an asset.

Ask yourself the following questions:

- What went wrong?

- How did it happen?

- When did it happen?

- Why did it happen?

- How could it have been prevented?

Once you have the answers to these questions, you will be able to adapt your actions in the future.

If Needed, Ask for Help

Overcoming your mistakes will require the help of your support system. An effective support system will include trust, diverse views, and mutual respect. The members of your support system can offer you advice and guidance. They will also provide valuable feedback that will show you how mistakes occurred and ways to avoid repeating the same errors.

Your support system will only be able to help you when you ask for it. You cannot expect people to automatically know when you need them. When you do ask for help, remember to follow basic etiquette.

- Ask: Do not demand that people help you or manipulate them with guilt.

- Be straightforward: Do not be dramatic or minimize the help necessary.

- Be thankful: Always thank friends who are willing to help you succeed.

Additional Titles

The 90 Minute Guide series of books covers a variety of general business skills and are intended to be completed in 90 minutes or less. It is an effective way for building your skill set and can be used to acquire professional development units needed by project managers and other industries to maintain their certification. For the availability of titles please see

https://www.silvercitypublications.com/shop/.

No. 1 - Appreciative Inquiry

No. 2 - Assertiveness and Self Control

No. 3 - Attention Management

No. 4 - Body Language Basics

No. 5 - Business Acumen

No. 6 - Business and Etiquette

No. 7 - Change Management

No. 8 - Coaching and Mentoring

No. 9 - Communications Strategies

No. 10 - Conflict Resolution

www.ingramcontent.com/pod-product-compliance
Lightning Source LLC
Chambersburg PA
CBHW060706280326
41933CB00012B/2322